sharing

sharing

Inspired recipes for office and home

Benoit Dewitte | Welkin & Meraki

LANNOO

STAUB

Table of Contents

Eat, work and enjoy as in a five-star hotel

Welkin and Meraki

Welkin & Meraki Eindhoven

Creation and magic: looking for a shareable workspace

When two visionary entrepreneurs, Alain Brossé and Benoit Dewitte, meet, there is always magic in the air, even if their activities are at first sight unrelated. And that is all the better, because craft and beauty are unbounded by limits and conventions. Just as cosmos has often arisen out of chaos, entrepreneurship is essentially the creation of something new, characterized by zeal and an urge for perfectionism.

Welkin and Meraki is the first worldwide provider of 'five-star serviced offices'. These are shared office spaces that are often known – not entirely correctly – as coworking spaces. CEO Alain Brossé: 'Coworking in the pure sense of the word implies that you share the workspace with others. But that is rarely the case in practice. SMEs and large companies need privacy and their own space, also within the larger whole of a serviced office.'

The Welkin and Meraki serviced offices

Brossé represents the crème de la crème when it comes to shared office space. As a director in the team of English billionaire Mark Dixon, he learned and then expanded the concept. 'Mark Dixon is the inventor of the serviced office. When he came to Brussels in 1989, his first intention was to set up a network of serviced apartments for the many European Union expats. During the weekend the apartment was cleaned, the refrigerator replenished, and suits taken to the dry cleaner. A brilliant idea. But when Mark himself wanted to rent a small 10 to 15 m² office from which to build up that activity, he found none. Mark had to sit in a 1,000 m² office as a one-man business!'

And in this way he changed from serviced apartments to serviced offices. The birth of Regus sent a shockwave through the dazed Brussels office landscape. Alain Brossé became its business development director for the Europe, Africa and Middle East regions. When he was then asked to develop Asia, he thought it was time for another challenge. He worked for Thomas Cook and co-founded Tribes, another well-known player in the coworking sector.

Finally in January 2018 he started Welkin and Meraki, which within months unleashed an unprecedented revolution. 'We want to move fast,' says Alain Brossé. 'In three years we hope to have fifty locations. Brussels, Luxembourg, Eindhoven and the two locations in Paris should, if all goes to plan, be followed by London, Shanghai, Amsterdam and Barcelona. In the United States, we are negotiating for different locations. Needless to say we are keen to have a strong presence in New York. In the longer term, Welkin and Meraki needs to become a company with no less than two hundred different locations.'

Only the very best is good enough

But what makes Welkin and Meraki so different from all

other serviced offices? The level, so it appears. Just as a five-star hotel does its utmost to pamper you 24/7, so a five-star serviced office must do everything it can to provide the companies renting space within it with every convenience. This starts with the hardware: the interior, the lighting, the decoration. Noble hardwood and sumptuous leather give a Welkin and Meraki office the cachet of a gentlemen's club. Interior architect Benoit Viaene received almost carte blanche to create a luxurious living room feeling. 'Our guests need to feel at home. Working here must relieve the pressure.'

The pursuit of perfection is expressed in invisible details. For example, every office has two separate internet connections. In this way, in the event of a network failure due to unforeseen roadworks or taking up of the pavement, one can immediately switch to the second internet entry point at the rear of the building.

The lighting is at 2,700 degrees Kelvin, unlike in regular offices, where 3,000-degree Kelvin lamps are standard. Alain Brossé: '3,000-degree lamps flicker. This is visible, for example, to migraine sufferers.'

Security is another important aspect, not least for the companies that rent temporary office space. Access is already protected by the most advanced system on the market, with codes that change every few nanoseconds.

But with Welkin and Meraki, perfection doesn't stop at design furniture and internet security. The whole picture must be right. For example, East Flanders' star chef Benoit Dewitte has been hired to look after the catering. Not only in Brussels, but worldwide. 'We want to give our guests the best of the best. And so Benoit set to work putting together an innovative and light breakfast and lunch menu. Every day we offer a healthy sharing lunch along with a number of fixed dishes.'

Coffee roaster Or blended an exclusive coffee for Welkin and Meraki from four different coffee beans. In each location, W&M has a barista who sees to it that every coffee runs for exactly 25 seconds, as do baristas in every self-respecting coffee house. 25 and not 24 or 26. Only then do you get the best coffee. The machines are re-adjusted every morning.

Welkin & Meraki Paris

Bringing people together creates happiness

Surely this level of service, this perfectionism, demands a high price? 'Five-star does not have to be expensive,' says Alain. 'Where possible, we open several locations at once. This reduces the cost of materials and equipment. A half-day pass is already possible from 35 euros, and if you stay a whole day, you pay 50 euros (75 euros in London and Paris) and with a Benoit Dewitte lunch thrown in. A monthly subscription to cowork every day can start from as little as 249 euros.' Welkin and Meraki is aimed in the first place not at young startups, but at large corporations and SMEs.

'But in the end everyone is welcome,' says Alain. 'We prefer long-term commitments and offer our guests all the facilities. Our business is all about people, it's a people business. We want to make people happy. Only in this way can you work efficiently and come across as relevant and authentic. For good reason, these are three of our key values.'

The hard training of a star chef

The art of cooking at star chef level is all about being able to give a signature to your dishes, a recognizability that sets you apart from your colleagues. That is what culinary guides

NATALYS
Best Mountain
GAP

Welkin & Meraki Paris

Benoit Dewitte

have in mind when they reward a chef for his excellence. In the case of Benoit Dewitte, it was quickly evident that his cuisine would carry a Provencal signature. Studies at the Ter Duinen hotel school in Koksijde were followed by an internship with the great Alain Ducasse at Moustiers in the south of France. 'Back then there was already an aura around Monsieur Ducasse, and our nerves were on edge whenever he came to check,' says Benoit. 'But even so, I retain good memories of that internship. It was a small kitchen team and the atmosphere was great. When my internship was over, I plucked up my courage and asked Monsieur Ducasse if he could arrange a place for me in Italy. That way I got to work for another three months with

Gualtiero Marchesi, the godfather of Italian nouvelle cuisine.'

But that's not what he was really cut out to do, and so Benoit returned to Provence for an internship at Wout Bru's Bistrot d'Eygalières. Then came L'Ousteau de Baumanière and L'Auberge de Noves, near Avignon. At the latter in particular he got to know the real Provencal cuisine. 'I stayed in Provence and ended up at Le Moulin de Lourmarin. That was one of the nicest stints, but also one of the toughest places to work in the kitchen. The chef, Edouard Loubet, was a Savoyard who had worked with the notorious Marc Veyrat. You know, Veyrat is the man in the black hat who started picking herbs in the mountains long before they came into use in Scandinavian cuisine. In Lourmarin I worked alongside Jean Sulpice, also a Savoyard. I learned a lot from him about herbs and infusions.'
Back in Belgium, two attractive proposals were waiting for the still very young East Fleming: a vacancy at the royal palace and a place at the Bruneau restaurant in Brussels, then a three-star restaurant. Benoit chose Bruneau, but had to start at the very bottom of the ladder. 'I said to myself: I'm 23, and by now I know how to do more than peel langoustines. After three days I left and returned home. There I started thinking about what I wanted to do with my life.'

Welkin & Meraki Brussels

Harmony at every level
Benoit Dewitte got his taste for good food and cooking from his mother, who cooks very well and likes standing behind a stove. To escape the stress of a restaurant, he started working as a caterer on a small scale. At his parental home in Zingem there was a stable that was no longer used. He converted it into a table d'hôte, with the flavours of the south. 'Those were the dishes I knew. I was sure it could be a success. Belgians like travelling to Provence and can absolutely appreciate the cuisine at its true value.'
Benoit quickly built up a reputation. Gault Millau proclaimed him the Best Young Chef in East Flanders. Soon after, Michelin came knocking at the door. But the inspector asked for a menu. 'We didn't have one. Twenty years ago you couldn't be included in the guide without a menu. Now all that has changed. In some starred restaurants today you have just one menu to choose from.'

Benoit's bother Bernard Dewitte and his wife Stephanie were eighteen when they came to help in the business during weekends. They slowly grew into the face of the business. This is how the restaurant evolved into what it is today: a modern auberge in the green fields of the Flemish Ardennes, with a special eye for aesthetics and architecture thanks to the input and savoir-faire of partner Geraldine Van Heuverswyn. The restaurant, bearing the name of the brothers, must be one of the most beautiful in Belgium. Large glass windows bring the impressive garden right up to the plate. Nothing is out of place inside, everything fits perfectly. Warm wood tones and ivory colours give a sense of calm. A great sense of harmony reigns at Benoit and Bernard Dewitte's.

Enter Welkin and Meraki

And then came the enquiry from Alain Brossé, CEO of Welkin and Meraki, asking whether Benoit was interested in catering for his new concept, not just in Belgium but worldwide. Benoit: 'Actually we were just starting to examine whether and how we might start a second business. It was a coincidence that I was evolving very fast towards sharing dishes. Healthy and light, with a focus on vegetables without becoming vegetarian or vegan. Of course I knew the concept of serviced offices, though I had no idea how we could fit a gastronomic component into it. But indeed today's culinary techniques are perfectly adapted to this type of gastronomy on location. We have opportunities today that were not around ten years ago. In Copenhagen, at the Restaurant Kadeau, I learned all about fermentation and pickling. These are simple techniques that we frequently use in the catering at Welkin and Meraki, and therefore also in this book. These flavours provide surprise and a fresh taste in a dish. I first sent my sous-chef to the first W&M location in Brussels to fine-tune everything. By now, we understand pretty much how it should be done, and how to adjust the logistics at other locations in the world to achieve the same result. At Welkin and Meraki, everything revolves around perfection. We cannot leave anything to chance. But the satisfaction afterwards is of course great.'

'In this book we will be sharing dishes right through the day, from breakfast to bedtime. With soups, salads and preparations that are playful, tasty and light. But especially super healthy and nutritious. These are the dishes that demanding businessmen and women taste in the Welkin and Meraki serviced offices. You can also make the same dishes at home, for your family, relatives or friends. Food is emotion. It brings people together round a table, whether in a five-star office or at your home.'

Sharing dishes

Breakfast

Granola, yoghurt, blueberry compote and pine oil

You can buy small pine trees in any garden shop. Ask for epicea conica. But if you can't find them, or you don't like the pine flavour, you can replace them with dried lavender.

- RECIPE FOR 10 LITTLE BOWLS -

150 g fresh Greek yoghurt per person
(i.e. 1.5 kg in total)
80 fresh blueberries for finishing
possibly some fresh mint leaves

For the blueberry compote:
500 g blueberries from the freezer
150 g sugar
juice and grated peel of 1 lemon
3 pieces star anise
grated peel of 1 lemon
4 g agar agar

For the pine oil:
1 small pine tree (epicea conica)
500 ml sunflower oil

For the granola:
250 g oatmeal
75 g hazelnuts, peeled and crushed
75 g almonds, peeled and crushed
75 g sunflower seeds
75 g pumpkin seeds
100 ml sunflower oil
120 g maple syrup
40 g honey
1 tablespoon brown sugar

Marinate the fruits with the sugar, lemon juice, lemon peel and star anise. Cook for 25 minutes on a low heat. Remove the star anise from the preparation and mix in a blender. Add the agar agar and boil again. Allow to cool and mix until smooth.
Mix all the ingredients for the granola together. Bake for 40 minutes at 160 °C in a preheated oven, stirring well every 10 minutes, then leave to cool.
Pick the twigs from the pine tree and mix with the oil in a Thermomix at 70 °C for 10 minutes. Alternatively, you can infuse the twigs in the oil for 30 minutes over a low heat.
Arrange the ingredients in the bowls: start with yoghurt, then 20 grams of compote, then 5 grams of pine oil and 40 grams of granola, and finally eight blueberries.
Possibly finish with some mint leaves.

Seasonal fruit, herb broth

What's in a name? A broth normally evokes images of soup, sauce and hearty meals, doesn't it? But replace the name with 'mocktail' and you immediately bring a summery atmosphere to the table with the same ingredients. Just add lots of ice cubes and fresh herbs like mint, verbena and basil. In this way, winter turns into summer.

- INGREDIENTS FOR 10 SMALL GLASSES -

You can vary the fruit according to season and availability. We always try to follow the seasons. Berries and strawberries are great in spring and summer, but mango and pineapple also work well in winter. Be careful with blackberries, as these discolour all other fruits.
Cut the fruit into bite-sized pieces and leave to soak in the broth for a whole day. The exact duration depends a bit on the discolouration and on what you find attractive.

For the bouillon:

1 litre water
200 g honey
50 g sugar
2 pieces star anise
1 cinnamon stick
1 lemongrass stalk
4 sprigs fresh sage
3 sprigs fresh mint
1 tablespoon dried lavender
grated peel of 1 lime and 1 orange
juice of 3 limes and 1 lemon

To finish:

grated peel of ½ lime
a few edible petals

Bring all the ingredients for the broth to the boil and leave to infuse for 15 minutes. Strain everything well and leave to cool. Add the fruit.
Compose each glass as follows: 150 grams of fruit, 40 grams of broth and finish with some grated lime peel and some petals.

Welkin & Meraki Paris

Fried egg, wild mushrooms, croutons, herb salad, mustard vinaigrette

There's nothing better to power you into a new day than an omelette or other egg preparation. Always try to add some vegetables to keep the balance. Here too the adage applies: stay with your season. While mushrooms can be used all year round, you can also replace them with white asparagus from April to June. Blanch these well before using.

- INGREDIENTS FOR 10 PEOPLE -

For the mustard vinaigrette:

150 g soft mustard
1 clove garlic, crushed
3 tablespoons sherry vinegar
Salt, sugar and pepper
1 dl of water
1 litre sunflower oil

For the croutons:

1 thick slice of white bread, diced
1 clove garlic
1 sprig rosemary
olive oil

For the herb salad:

Reckon on around 30 grams per person. Here you can use young rocket, leaf parsley, dill, young red sorrel, chervil and chives.
You don't necessarily need all of these.
Choose what you like yourself according to your own taste.

And also:

80 g wild mushrooms per person
1 knob of butter and garlic oil (see basic recipe p. 174)
pepper and salt
2 eggs per person

Mix the ingredients for the vinaigrette in a blender and work up with the oil.
Bake the pieces of white bread in olive oil with a clove of garlic and a sprig of rosemary until nicely crispy.
Fry 80 grams of mushrooms in a knob of butter with garlic oil.
Season with pepper and salt.
Fry two eggs in a pan. The eggs must fit exactly in the pan.
Season the yolk with a pinch of salt and cook until the egg white is tender.
Serve with the mushrooms, finish with the herb salad and sprinkle with some mustard vinaigrette and with the croutons.

Boule de Berlin

I drew my inspiration for this recipe from the famous 'Tarte Tropézienne', or filled brioche. This pastry was originally designed as a dessert, but as we all know, a breakfast buffet is not complete without cakes and other sweet things. The Tarte Tropézienne was created in 1955 by pastry cook Alexandre Micka in honour of Brigitte Bardot, who was staying that year in the fashionable French seaside resort to film Et Dieu créa la femme (1956, Roger Vadim).

- INGREDIENTS FOR 30 SMALL BOULES -

For the batter:

230 ml whole milk
30 g fresh yeast
500 g flour
60 g butter (at room temperature)
145 g vanilla sugar
6 g salt
neutral oil (such as peanut oil) for greasing

For the pastry cream:

1 litre whole milk
120 g egg yolks
100 g pudding mix
120 g sugar
1 vanilla pod
50 g butter
a pinch of orange blossom

To finish:

icing sugar
grated peel of 1 lemon

Heat the milk until lukewarm. Dissolve the fresh yeast in it.
Put the flour, butter, salt and vanilla sugar in the food processor bowl. Run the food processor until everything is well mixed.
Slowly pour in the milk with the yeast and knead into an elastic dough in the food processor. It must not stick, but must not be too dry either.
Preheat the oven to 30 °C.
Rub a large bowl with a lick of neutral oil and dust with flour.
Lay the dough in it and cover with a clean kitchen towel.
Leave the dough to rise for 40 minutes in the lightly heated oven.
Meanwhile, prepare the pastry cream. Bring the milk to the boil. Beat the egg yolks, the pudding powder, the sugar and the vanilla together. Combine with the boiling milk. Mix into a sauce. Now stir the butter into the mixture and leave everything to cool.
Beat with a pinch of orange blossom to taste.
Remove the risen dough from the oven and push the air out. Knead briefly once again and then form balls larger than golf balls but smaller than tennis balls.
Cover a baking tray with baking paper or place a silicon mat on it. Place the balls on the baking tray with sufficient space between them and cover with a towel.
Leave for another 20 minutes in the oven at 30 °C to rise.
Heat the deep fryer to 170 °C.
Bake the balls golden brown all over in the frying oil.
Halfway through the frying time turn with a spoon.
Place on kitchen paper to drain and leave to cool.
Inject the cooled pastry cream into the boules and finish with icing sugar and grated lemon peel.

Charcuterie with homemade pickles and sourdough bread

In this recipe, you will learn how to make pickles or pickled vegetables yourself. You can buy the sourdough bread from a better bakery, and the charcuterie from the butcher. Be guided here by your taste: dried or cooked ham, bresaola, filet d'Anvers, but also all kinds of tasty pâtés or rillettes go excellently with pickles.

Ingredients for three 1-litre preserving jars:

1 kg mix of radishes, shallots, carrots, celery and red onions, cut into pieces and washed
1 litre water
1 litre white vinegar
600 g sugar
3 sprigs fresh thyme
3 bay leaves
20 g peppercorns
3 garlic cloves, crushed with the skin

Divide the vegetables over the three jars and add the aromatics.
For the brine, boil the water, vinegar and sugar and pour over the vegetables.
Close and leave to cool.
Wait at least 1 week before serving.
Cut the charcuterie paper-thin and serve with fresh farm butter,
the pickles and a healthy slice of sourdough bread.
After opening, store the pickles in the refrigerator.

Soups

Tomato soup, mascarpone, basil and roasted seeds

Some soups lend themselves perfectly for serving both hot and cold. In the summer you can equally well serve this tomato soup ice-cold as a kind of gazpacho.

For the soup:

2 kg fresh ripe tomatoes
500 g sweet pointed peppers
800 g Spanish onion
2 garlic cloves, crushed
2 sprigs basil
olive oil
500 g poultry bouillon
1 tablespoon sugar
3 tablespoons chicken bouillon (in powder form)
pepper and salt

For the mascarpone:

200 g mascarpone
20 g pickled shallot (see basic recipe p. 174)
20 g fresh herbs, chopped (mint, tarragon, chervil, chives)

For the seed mix:

30 g pumpkin seeds
30 g sunflower seeds
30 g sesame seeds

And also:

basil oil
(see basic recipe p. 175)
fresh basil to finish

Stew all the ingredients for the soup in olive oil for 15 minutes and then add the bouillon.
Add the sugar and the chicken bouillon powder and leave to simmer slowly for 30 minutes. Mix well and season with salt and pepper.
Mix the ingredients for the mascarpone.
Roast the seeds until crispy at 150 °C.
Finish the soup with a scoop of the mascarpone mixture, a splash of basil oil, roasted seeds and a few tufts of fresh basil.

Onion soup, sourdough croutons, Gruyère cheese and basil oil

10 Spanish onions, sliced
2 garlic cloves, crushed
1 bunch thyme
a few bay leaves
olive oil
sugar
2 dl white wine
4 litres chicken bouillon
2 dl olive oil
pepper and salt

To finish:

200 g grated Gruyère
basil oil
20 g sourdough croutons per person
a few sprigs of leaf parsley or chervil

Colour the onions together with the garlic, thyme and the bay leaves in a dash of olive oil and leave to simmer for 30 minutes.
Add some sugar, deglaze with the wine and the chicken bouillon.
Cook till soft. Remove the thyme and the bay leaves, mix and strain the soup.
Season with salt and pepper.
Finish with the grated cheese, basil oil, sourdough croutons and some tufts of leaf parsley or chervil.

Pumpkin soup, coconut foam, roasted seeds and lemongrass oil

For the pumpkin soup:

2 bottleneck pumpkins, diced
2 large carrots, peeled and cut into rounds
2 garlic cloves, peeled and crushed
2 Spanish onions, cut into small pieces
1 'golden' apple, cut into small pieces
3 tablespoons soft curry powder
3 dl cream
1 lemongrass stalk, finely chopped
olive oil
3 litres chicken bouillon
possibly some chicken bouillon powder
pepper and salt

For the coconut foam:

½ bell pepper, finely chopped
1 garlic clove, peeled and crushed
1 Spanish onions, diced
2 lemongrass stalks, finely chopped
4 lime leaves
10 sprigs coriander
1 tablespoon chicken bouillon powder
olive oil
1 dl lemongrass and ginger vinegar (basic recipe see p. 174)
1 litre coconut milk
juice of 1 lime

For the lemongrass oil:

1 litre sunflower oil
10 lemongrass stalks
1 garlic clove
1 bell pepper, chopped into pieces
20 g ginger, peeled
20 g lime leaves

For the seeds (20 g per person):

pumpkin seeds
sunflower seeds
sesame seeds

To finish:

some flowers,
coriander leaves,
grated lime peel

Stew all the ingredients for the soup gently in a saucepan with some olive oil and then moisten with the chicken bouillon.
Bring to the boil, allow everything to cook well, mix and pour through a sieve.
Season with pepper and salt.
Stew the dry ingredients for the coconut foam in some oil and deglaze with the vinegar. Add the coconut milk and the chicken bouillon powder and reduce by half.
Pour through a sieve and add some lime juice.
Mix the ingredients for the lemongrass oil for 10 minutes at 70 °C in a Thermomix or in a regular blender. Pour through a fine sieve.
Roast the seeds in the oven at 150 °C.
Serve the soup with a little coconut foam, a dash of lemongrass oil and some roasted seeds. Finish with small flowers, coriander leaves and/or grated lime peel.

Asparagus broth with savory, pea ravioli, ricotta and bacon

For the broth:

3 kg green (or white) asparagus peelings (you can use the peelings from the baked asparagus recipe, see p. 104)
1 kg onions, in mirepoix
2 garlic cloves, crushed
100 g fresh savory, tied together with string
100 g butter
1 dl white wine
4 litres chicken bouillon
1 tablespoon chicken bouillon powder
1 litre cream
pepper and salt

For the ravioli filling:

200 g Spanish onion, diced
50 ml olive oil
100 g smoked bacon, in thick slices
50 g fresh thyme, in a tuft
500 g peas (frozen)
1 dl white wine
pepper and salt
200 g fresh spinach, blanched and squeezed
1 kg ricotta, drained
200 g parmesan, grated
½ nutmeg, grated
2 eggs
2 garlic cloves, crushed

For the ravioli dough:

see basic recipe on p.80

To finish:

50 g onion, in strips
1 garlic clove, shredded
olive oil
salt and pepper
200 g peas
a herb salad (dill, mint, tarragon)

First make the broth. Fry all the solid ingredients in a cooking pot with butter and allow to sweat.
Deglaze with the white wine and the chicken bouillon, add the chicken bouillon powder and then the cream.
Leave to simmer gently for 1 hour. Remove the savory from the broth, strain and season. Now prepare the ravioli.
Fry the onions in the oil with the bacon and thyme and leave to sweat.
Add the peas and deglaze with the wine.
Leave to simmer and season with salt and pepper.
Cut the spinach roughly and add to the pan. Mix everything in a blender.
Now mix the ricotta, parmesan and nutmeg into the mixture, add the eggs, mix well again and season with salt and pepper.
Fry the onions and garlic for the finishing and season to taste.
Add the peas and leave to cook for a while.
Serve together with the ravioli and the broth, and finish with the herb salad.

Bread

-

Toast

Marinated salmon, seed bread, potato, dill and cucumber

This is a true classic of Norwegian cuisine. I prepare it as a light and nutritious lunch. There is no precise rule for how much grated peel or horseradish to add. Some prefer it spicier, others can just leave out the horseradish. Feel free to play with the preparation.

- INGREDIENTS TO SERVE 10 -

For the salmon:

80 g salmon per person
generous dash of olive oil
grated lime peel
fresh horseradish, finely grated
pepper and salt

For the cucumber:

500 g cucumber, in thin slices
salt
30 g dill, freshly chopped
10 g red peppercorns
3 g coriander seeds, bruised
100 g shallot, finely shredded
500 g brine (see basic recipe p. 174)

For the dill emulsion:

1 litre sunflower oil
1 clove garlic, crushed
50 g fresh dill
75 g mustard
200 g egg white
80 g dill vinegar
pepper and salt

For the potato slices:

a few baby new potatoes
olive oil
pepper
coarse salt

And also:

10 slices of seed bread, 1.5 cm thick
pickled mustard seeds
some finely shredded shallot as a garnish
fresh dill

Cut the salmon into thin slices. Marinate with the olive oil, grated lime peel and grated horseradish, and season with pepper and salt.

Season the cucumber slices with salt and leave to drain for 20 minutes in a sieve. Rinse thoroughly under water until all the salt has been removed.

Mix with the herbs and shallot and pour the brine onto the cucumber preparation. Store in the refrigerator.

Mix all the ingredients for the dill emulsion in the blender, except the oil. Slowly pour in the sunflower oil and bind into an emulsion.

Cook the unpeeled baby potatoes in salt water until al dente and leave to cool. Peel and slice the potatoes. Drizzle with some olive oil and season with pepper and coarse salt.

Cover each slice of bread with salmon, cucumber and potato slices. Finish with the emulsion and possibly some pickled mustard seeds (see basic recipe p. 172) and shallot. Garnish with fresh dill.

Sourdough toast with beef carpaccio, rocket and parmesan

For the truffle emulsion:

2 garlic cloves, crushed
50 g truffle juice
20 ml truffle oil
75 g mustard
50 ml water
200 g egg white
70 ml sherry vinegar
pepper and salt
pinch of sugar
1 litre sunflower oil

For the shallot rings:

shallots
brine (see basic recipe p. 174)

For the basil oil:

1 bunch basil (only the leaves)
1 litre sunflower oil
2 cloves garlic, crushed

For the carpaccio:

60 g beef carpaccio per person
Maldon salt
pepper from the mill

And further:

20 g rocket per person
1 slice sourdough bread per person, 2 cm thick

For the finishing:

parmesan, finely grated
truffle oil
grated lime peel
a few young basil leaves

Mix all the ingredients for the emulsion, except the oil, in the blender until smooth. Slowly pour in the sunflower oil and bind with the mixture.

Peel the shallots and cut into thin rings. Bring the brine to the boil and pour it hot on the shallot rings. Leave to cool in the refrigerator.

Mix the ingredients for the basil oil very finely in a blender and store in the refrigerator.

Grill the sourdough bread slices on both sides and brush the emulsion over the entire toast.

Season the rocket with basil oil, balsamic vinegar, pepper and salt, and spread on the toast.

Then arrange the carpaccio on the toast and season with salt and pepper.

Finally, arrange five shallot rings on the meat and finish with grated parmesan, truffle oil, grated lime peel and young basil.

Brioche with pulled pork and smoked bell pepper

- 1 BRIOCHE PER PERSON -

For the pulled pork:

1 good quality pork shoulder, boned, approx. 3 kg
500 ml apple juice
juice of 1 lime

For the marinade:

3 garlic cloves, peeled
6 sprigs fresh thyme, finely chopped
2 dl thyme pickling brine (see basic recipe p. 174)
1 dl soy sauce
4 tablespoons smoked paprika powder
1 tablespoon cumin and aniseed
1 shallot, diced
1 litre sunflower oil

For the smoked paprika sauce:

2 garlic cloves, crushed
15 g smoked paprika powder
75 g mustard
200 g egg white
80 ml sherry vinegar
pepper and salt
1 litre sunflower oil

For the coleslaw:

200 g finely chopped white or Chinese cabbage
50 g cashew nuts, roasted without salt
20 leaves and tufts of fresh coriander and mint
splash of thyme vinegar (see basic recipe p. 174)
olive oil
grated lime peel
pepper and salt

Mix the ingredients for the marinade finely in a blender.
Place the meat in a baking dish, pour over the marinade and then the apple juice. Leave to marinate overnight in the refrigerator.
The next day preheat the oven to 140 °C and cover the meat with a lid or foil.
Cook in the oven for 4 to 5 hours until the meat falls apart nicely.
Divide the meat into tufts and season with the gravy and some lime juice.
Mix all the ingredients for the smoked paprika emulsion, except the oil, in the blender until smooth.
Slowly pour in the sunflower oil and bind into a smooth emulsion.
Mix the ingredients for the coleslaw and season with thyme vinegar, olive oil, grated lime peel, pepper and salt.
Cut open the brioche, place the meat on the lower half, cover with coleslaw, and finish with the smoked paprika sauce.

Seed bread with radishes and yoghurt, lime, black olive and za'atar

Za'atar is a spice mixture from the Middle East. Traditionally, it consists of the spice itself, mixed with sesame seeds and sumac, another fresh-sour spice from the Levant cuisine. The mixture is eaten with both meat and vegetable dishes or, as in Israel and in the Palestinian territories, for breakfast on a sandwich with olive oil.

1 slice seed bread per person, 1.5 cm thick
50 g Greek yoghurt per person
4 fresh radishes per person, sliced

For the radish pickle:

20 radishes
brine
(see basic recipe p. 174)

For the basil oil:

see basic recipe p. 175

To finish:

tapenade of black olives (natural, commercially available)
za'atar spice mix
grated lime peel
some tarragon leaves
basil, dill, tarragon and small flowers

Bring the brine to the boil and pour over the cleaned radishes.
Leave to cool and store in a cool place.
Cover the slices of bread with a layer of yoghurt.
Arrange the pieces and add slices of fresh and pickled radish on top.
Finish with some tapenade, za'atar and finally with some tufts and leaves of tarragon, basil and dill.
Garnish with basil oil, grated lime peel and petals.

RESTAURANT

'Brioche' club sandwich

4 brioche rolls
1 chicken fillet
1 tablespoon yoghurt
1 pinch garlic powder, cumin, curry powder, ginger powder
pepper and salt

To finish:

4 thinly sliced strips of smoked bacon, baked crisp
4 slices ripe tomato
4 iceberg lettuce leaves
8 basil leaves
50 g parmesan, grated
1 hard-boiled egg, cut into 4

For the sauce:

We use our basil emulsion here (see basic recipe p. 175).

Prepare the marinade with yoghurt and spices and marinate the chicken in it overnight.
Cook the fillet the next day for 30 minutes at 62 °C.
Fry the bacon on the grill and cut into slices.
Make a sandwich in the same way as a club sandwich, with slices of chicken, bacon, vegetables and herbs, egg and parmesan. Serve the basil emulsion as a sauce.

Toast with fresh cheese, savory, aubergine and tomato

- INGREDIENTS FOR 10 TOASTS-

1 focaccia-type bread, in 10 slices
1 garlic clove, peeled

For the aubergine:

4 aubergines, cut in half and notched
1 dl olive oil
4 sprigs thyme and rosemary
8 garlic cloves, bruised
20 g olive tapenade
20 ml basil oil (see basic recipe p. 175)
20 ml balsamic vinegar
pepper and salt

For the tomatoes:

10 cherry tomatoes, peeled and halved
mint vinegar (see basic recipe p. 174)
basil oil
grated peel of 1 lime
Maldon sea salt and pepper

For the cheese:

250 g fresh goat cheese, without crust
3 g pickled shallot
5 sprigs savory
1 dl olive oil
pepper and salt

To finish:

basil, mint, coriander and little flowers

Sprinkle the aubergines with olive oil and place the aromatics on the aubergine.
Season with pepper and salt.
Bake in a preheated oven at 180 °C for 35 minutes.
Remove the flesh from the aubergines with a spoon, leave to drain in a sieve and chop finely.
Season with the olive tapenade, oil and vinegar and keep cool.
Season the tomatoes with the aromatics.
Toast the focaccia and rub with a clove of garlic.
Mix the goat cheese well with the shallot, the savory and the olive oil,
and season with salt and pepper.
Place the cheese on the toast, lay the aubergine on the cheese
and distribute the tomatoes over the dish.
Garnish with some herbs and little flowers.

Toast with courgette, fresh ricotta, lime and spinach

1 slice sourdough bread per person

For the courgette:

2 courgettes, cut into equal 3 x 3 cm pieces
olive oil
1 garlic clove, crushed
1 tablespoon ginger powder
pepper and salt
1 tablespoon honey
juice and grated peel of 1 lime
20 g coriander, chopped

For the ricotta:

500 g ricotta, drained
200 g spinach, cooked and mashed (in a blender)
1 garlic clove, crushed
1 dl olive oil
juice and grated peel of 3 limes
300 g parmesan, grated
½ nutmeg, grated
pepper and salt

To finish:

basil oil (see basic recipe p. 175)
fresh coriander
tapenade of green olives

Lightly fry the courgette in olive oil.
Add the garlic. Season with ginger, pepper and salt.
Continue to fry until lightly coloured and add the honey. Leave to simmer until the courgette is cooked.
Deglaze with the lime juice, then finish with the grated peel and fresh coriander.
Toast the bread on one side.
Blend all the ingredients for the ricotta together and season.
Spread the ricotta on the toast.
Lay the courgette on the ricotta and sprinkle with basil oil and fresh coriander.
Finish with the tapenade.

Raw

Beef carpaccio, candied tomato, pine nuts and tarragon

100 g beef fillet per person, thinly sliced

For the basil emulsion:

80 g mustard
100 g fresh basil
20 ml sherry vinegar
pinch of sugar
200 g egg white
50 ml water
2 garlic cloves, crushed
1 litre sunflower oil
pepper and salt

For the tomato salsa:

4 tomatoes, peeled and with the flesh removed
pinch of sugar
pepper and salt
4 garlic cloves
6 sprigs thyme
1 dl olive oil
50 g roasted pine nuts
30 g fresh tarragon, finely chopped
30 g pickled shallot, in small pieces
30 ml veal jus (see basic recipe p. 177)

To finish:

some basil leaves and coriander flowers

Mix all the ingredients for the emulsion, except the oil, in the blender. Slowly pour in the sunflower oil and bind, then season to taste.
Marinate the tomatoes with the sugar, pepper and salt, garlic, thyme and olive oil.
Candy the tomatoes in the oven at 90 °C for 3 hours.
Finely chop the tomatoes and mix with the pine nuts, tarragon and shallot.
Add the veal jus and season.
Spread some basil sauce on the plate, arrange the beef slices on the sauce and finish with the tomato salsa. Garnish with basil leaves and coriander flowers.

Salmon carpaccio with pink pepper and chives

100 g fresh raw salmon
per person, finely
chopped
pepper and salt
50 g chives, finely
chopped
10 g pink peppercorns
a few drops of good
balsamic vinegar
30 g shallot, finely
shredded
1 dl good quality olive oil

To finish:

sourdough croutons

Season the salmon with pepper and salt.
Sprinkle some chives and pink pepper over the salmon.
Make a vinaigrette with the balsamic vinegar, shallot and the olive oil and marinate the salmon for a few minutes before serving.
Finish with small croutons.

Ceviche of sea bream, coconut, mint, coriander and avocado

For the sea bream:

4 fillets of king sea bream, approx. 100 g per fillet
pepper and salt
grated peel of 1 lime
lemongrass oil (see basic recipe p. 172)

For the avocado crème:

3 avocados
1 shallot, finely shredded
2 dl olive oil
1 dl mint vinegar (see basic recipe p. 174)grated peel and juice of 1 lime
½ garlic clove, crushed
5 sprigs fresh coriander
pepper and salt

For the jus:

500 ml coconut milk
1 small chilli pepper
2 shallots, shredded
3 sprigs mint and coriander, finely chopped
1 dl mint vinegar
50 g ginger, chopped
200 g Greek yoghurt
grated peel and juice of 2 limes
heads and bones of the fish
pepper and salt
leek oil (see basic recipe p. 174)
lemongrass oil

To finish:

some roasted and chopped peanuts
pickled shallots (see basic recipe p. 174)
fresh coriander leaves
flowers and herbs
grated lime peel

Skin the fish fillets and cut away the red part in the middle of the fillet.
Cut the fish into equal chunks and season with salt and pepper,
the grated lime peel and the lemongrass oil.
Do this just before serving so that the fish does not cook prematurely because of the acids.
Mix the avocados with the other ingredients into a smooth crème and season with salt and pepper.
Mix all the ingredients for the jus, except for the fish heads and bones, in a blender. Add the heads and bones and leave the sauce to marinate for 2 to 3 hours in the refrigerator. Pour through a fine sieve and season to taste. Finish with leek oil and some lemongrass oil.
Place the avocado cream in a deep plate. Place the fish on the cream. Finish with the roasted peanuts, pickled shallot, coriander, flowers and herbs, and the grated lime peel.

Gillardeau oyster with cucumber, lemongrass and chilli

For the cucumber emulsion:

1 litre cucumber juice
4 gelatine leaves
5 sprigs fresh mint
40 g glucose
1 dl mint pickle
juice of 1 lime
3 g albumen (egg white powder)
50 g pro espuma (a stabilizer for cold preparations)
pepper and salt

For the oyster marinade:

2 dl lemongrass and ginger pickle
2 tablespoons oyster sauce
50 g shallot, finely shredded
a pinch of fresh chilli
2 dl lemongrass oil (see basic recipe p. 172)
30 g coriander, finely chopped
juice of 1 lime
10 Gillardeau oysters, open (you can ask the fishmonger to do this if you have no experience with opening oysters yourself. It's always a messy job.)

To finish:

grated peel of 1 lime
a handful of roasted sesame seeds

First make a litre of cucumber juice with a juicer.
Heat up a small portion of the cucumber juice and add the soaked gelatine leaves.
Mix the rest of the juice with the mint, glucose, pickle, albumen and the pro espuma. Season with salt and pepper and place the smaller portion of juice into an espuma bottle with two gas cartridges.
Mix the ingredients for the marinade. Marinate the oysters in the marinade. Add the cucumber emulsion and finish with grated lime peel and roasted sesame seeds.

Pasta

Soba noodles, dashi vinaigrette and fried shiitake mushrooms

For the dashi vinaigrette:

600 ml water
100 ml light soy sauce
100 ml lime juice
20 g brown sugar
50 g ginger and lemongrass pickling brine (see basic recipe p. 172)
50 g fresh coriander
2 lemongrass stalks
1 small chilli pepper, finely chopped
60 g tuna flakes
5 shallots, shredded
2 garlic cloves, crushed
10 g sesame oil
200 g lemongrass oil

For the noodles:

500 g cooked soba noodles
100 g cashew nuts, roasted and bruised (30 minutes at 150 °C)
50 g sesame seeds, roasted

For the vegetables:

200 g fresh mini shiitake mushrooms
5 mini bok choy, cut into pieces
5 shallots, in half rings
2 garlic cloves, bruised
1 dl oriental oil
handful of edamame beans

To finish:

a few tufts of coriander and mint
flower petals
grated lime peel

Bring the water to the boil with the soy sauce, lime juice, sugar, pickling brine, coriander, lemongrass, shallots, garlic and chilli pepper.
Add the tuna flakes and simmer for 10 minutes on a low heat.
Strain and leave to cool. Add the oil and season.
Mix the soba noodles with the nuts and seeds and season with the dashi vinaigrette.
Stir fry the vegetables in a hot pan with the garlic and oil. Season with pepper and salt. Add to the noodles, and finish with the beans.
Arrange everything together in a large bowl and finish with fresh-plucked coriander and mint, petals and grated lime peel.

Ricotta ravioli with lime and spinach, grilled leek and parmesan

A highly original and relatively simple vegetarian pasta dish.

For the dough:

800 g durum wheat flour, type 00
200 g semolina
900 g egg yolk
100 ml water
5 g salt
10 ml vinegar

For the sauce:

500 ml milk
500 ml cream
300 g parmesan, grated
150 g egg white
pepper and salt
nutmeg

For the filling:

500 g ricotta, drained
250 g spinach, cooked and pureed (in the blender)
2 garlic cloves, crushed
grated peel and juice of 3 limes
200 g parmesan, grated
½ nutmeg, grated
2 small eggs
pepper and salt

To finish:

some leek strands, browned in some olive oil
a good balsamic vinegar
basil oil (see basic recipe p. 175)
grated parmesan

Mix the ingredients for the dough and leave to rest in the refrigerator for 3 hours. In the meantime, make the filling by mixing all the ingredients. Roll out the dough thinly and fill with the filling. Finally prepare the sauce. Heat the milk and cream and add the grated parmesan. Melt the ricotta, pour through a sieve, add the egg white and season with pepper, salt and nutmeg.
Put the sauce in a kidde (spray can) with two gas cartridges and heat to 70 °C. If you don't have one in the house, you can do without it. Then omit the protein and simply heat the sauce in a pan.
Cook the ravioli al dente for 4 minutes in salted water.
Finish with some leek strands, vinegar and basil oil and some grated parmesan.

Welkin & Meraki Brussels

SURF
PHOTOGRAPHY
Rome

Ravioli with chicken, tom kha gai, shiitake and cashew nuts

This pasta preparation was inspired by my trip to fabulous Thailand, where you will find one of the tastiest and at the same time healthiest cuisines in the world. Tom kha gai is traditionally a classic spicy-sour chicken soup with coconut milk.

For the dough:

see basic recipe on p. 177

For the sauce:

½ chilli pepper
1 garlic clove
800 g Spanish onion
1 tablespoon chicken bouillon powder
2 lemongrass stalks
4 lime leaves
10 sprigs coriander
1 dl oriental vinegar
1 litre coconut milk
1 lime

For the filling:

500 g chicken breast or finely ground prawn tails
100 g coriander, finely chopped
100 g white of leek, finely chopped
100 g carrots, finely chopped
100 g shallot, shredded
3 tablespoons oyster sauce
2 tablespoons soy sauce
1 garlic clove, crushed
40 g ginger, finely chopped
2 tablespoons sesame oil
juice of 1 lime
grated peel of 2 limes
2 eggs

For the vegetables:

200 g fresh mini shiitake mushrooms
5 mini bok choy, cut into pieces
5 shallots, shredded
2 garlic cloves, bruised
1 dl lemongrass oil
pepper and salt
150 g edamame beans
grated peel of 2 limes

To finish:

cashew nuts
fresh coriander

Prepare the dough as in the recipe on p. 80.
Lightly fry the ingredients for the sauce and deglaze with the vinegar. Add the coconut milk and reduce by half. Press through a sieve and add some lime juice.
Stir fry the vegetables in a hot pan with the garlic and oil. Season with pepper and salt. Finish with the beans and grated lime peel.
Mix all the ingredients for the filling together and fill the ravioli.
Cook the ravioli al dente for 4 minutes in salted water.
Serve the ravioli with the sauce and the vegetables, and finish with a few cashew nuts and possibly some tufts of coriander.

Pumpkin ravioli, bisque and candied carrots

For the dough:

see basic recipe on p. 177

For the bisque:

3 kg shrimp heads
olive oil for frying
400 g shallot, cut into pieces
3 garlic cloves, crushed
50 g fresh thyme
2 dl pastis
1 dl white wine
5 litre chicken stock
250 g butter, unsalted (to work up the sauce)
1 carrot, peeled and cut into rounds
1 fennel, cut into pieces

For the carrots:

50 g chicken stock
50 g fresh butter
1 garlic clove, crushed
20 young carrots, blanched and without leaves
50 g fresh herbs, finely chopped (e.g. dill, coriander and parsley)
pepper and salt

For the pumpkin filling:

500 g pumpkin, de-seeded and cut into chunks
1 dl olive oil
250 g onion, chopped into small chunks
2 garlic cloves, crushed
1 tablespoon curry
1 tablespoon cumin powder
1 teaspoon cinnamon powder
3 tablespoons soft flower honey
juice of 1 lime
6 sprigs of fresh thyme, sage and rosemary (mixed)
200 g parmesan, grated
pepper and salt

Make a dough as in the basic recipe on p. 80.
Lightly fry the shrimp carcasses in olive oil and add the shallot, carrot, fennel, garlic and thyme. Leave to simmer.
Deglaze with the pastis and the white wine and moisten with the stock.
Leave to cook gently for 1 hour, then pour through a sieve.
Reduce to sauce thickness and finish with the butter.
Season with pepper and salt and beat to a foam before serving.
Now prepare the carrots. Reduce the stock and the butter with the garlic. Add the carrots and glaze.
Finish with the herbs and season with salt and pepper.
Mix all the ingredients for the filling together, except the cheese, and bake for 30 minutes in a preheated oven at 180 °C until everything is cooked and caramelized. Mix in a blender, leave to cool and then mix in the cheese. Season with salt and pepper.
Fill the ravioli with the pumpkin filling and cook al dente for 4 minutes.
Serve with the carrots and the bisque.

Cold and hot salads
-
Side dishes

Crispy vegetable with anchovy and lovage dip

Dreamy, lazy summers require spicy touches. In Provence, and by extension throughout south-east France, an anchoïade is a delicious dip made from the best anchovies, the best olive oil, vinegar and garlic. Traditionally, anchoïade is eaten with southern vegetables such as red pepper, fennel or snow peas.

Ingredients for 1 litre of dip:

2 garlic cloves, crushed
10 sprigs fresh lovage (or basil as an alternative)
7 anchovies, in oil
2 tablespoons mustard
1 dl water
200 g egg white
pinch of sugar
fresh-ground pepper
3 tablespoons sherry vinegar
1 litre sunflower oil

And further:

seasonal vegetables: celery, carrots, cauliflower, cherry tomatoes, radishes ...

This recipe is very simple: mix all the ingredients for the dip, except the oil, in a blender until smooth. Pour in the oil slowly and bind as you would a mayonnaise.

Leek fritter with a leek and tarragon emulsion

3 leeks (white part only)

For the fritter batter:

250 ml blond beer
200 g trisol (soluble wheat fibre, ideal for deep-frying)
300 g flour

For the leek and tarragon emulsion:

1 litre leek oil (see basic recipe p. 174)
80 g mustard
50 g tarragon vinegar
30 ml water
2 garlic cloves
50 g fresh tarragon
pepper and salt

Mix the beer, trisol and flour into a batter. Pour into an espuma bottle with two gas cartridges.
Cut the leek into rings 1 cm thick.
Roll the rings in the fritter batter and fry at 180 °C until golden brown. Mix the emulsion ingredients in a blender, pour in the leek oil slowly and bind. Season with pepper and salt.
Serve the leek fritters with the sauce.

Roasted pumpkin, raisins, hazelnut vinaigrette, bulgur and yoghurt

For the pumpkin:

1/2 pumpkin, de-seeded and cut into 3 x 5 cm chunks
2 tablespoons honey
2 teaspoons cumin, ras el hanout, curry powder (mixed)
2 garlic cloves, crushed with peel
3 sprigs fresh thyme, sage and rosemary (mixed)
1 Spanish onion, peeled and sliced
2 dl olive oil
pepper and salt
juice of 2 limes
some fresh coriander leaves to finish

For the nut vinaigrette:

3 dl reduced veal jus (see basic recipe p. 177)
1 tablespoon dry sherry and port (mixed)
3 tablespoons sherry vinegar
2 tablespoons shallot, finely shredded
1 sprig fresh thyme
a few bay leaves
1 garlic clove, bruised
pepper and salt
4 tablespoons roasted hazelnuts, chopped
1 dl hazelnut oil
1 dl olive oil
1 dl sunflower oil

For the pickled raisins:

1 kg white raisins
1.5 litres basic brine (see basic recipe p.174)

For the yoghurt preparation:

500 g Greek yoghurt
3 tablespoons pickled shallot (see basic recipe p. 174)
pepper and salt
a few leaves of fresh mint and coriander
1 teaspoon sumac
basil oil (see recipe p. 175)

For the bulgur salad:

500 g bulgur
2 litres fresh vegetable bouillon (from the skins of the vegetables)
3 tablespoons cumin
1 pickled lemon on salt (for tajine)
2 garlic cloves, crushed
1 cinnamon stick
2 dl olive oil
grated peel of 2 lemons
3 tablespoons brunoise of pickled onions
50 g parsley, chopped
50 g coriander, chopped
juice of 1 lemon

For the basil oil:

1 bunch basil (leaves only)
1 litre sunflower oil
2 garlic cloves, crushed

And further:

some peeled hazelnuts
herb salad: a mixture of young rocket, leaf parsley, dill, young red sorrel, chervil, chives and coriander (to taste).

Mix the pumpkin chunks with all the herbs, spices and condiments and bake in a baking dish at 180 °C for 25 minutes. Leave to cool and finish with some coriander leaves.

Cook the bulgur in the vegetable bouillon with the cumin, lemon, garlic and cinnamon. Drain and leave to cool. Remove the cinnamon stick from the preparation. Finish with the oil, grated lemon peel, lemon juice, onions and chopped parsley and coriander.

Soak the raisins in water overnight. Boil the brine and pour it over the raisins. Leave to cool.

Now prepare the vinaigrette. Briefly bring the veal jus, sherry, port, sherry vinegar, shallot, thyme, bay leaf and garlic to the boil and season with salt and pepper. Remove from the heat. Add hazelnuts and the oils, and season. Serve lukewarm.

Mix the basil with the sunflower oil and garlic very finely in a blender and store in the refrigerator.

Mix the yoghurt with the pickled shallot and season with salt and pepper. Finish with fresh mint and coriander, sumac and basil oil.

Colour the hazelnuts briefly in the oven and chop into large pieces.

Serve everything together with a herb salad.

'Gado gado' beans

This is a really spicy bean salad that I tasted for the first time on the Indonesian island of Bali. I was then guest chef at the Viceroy Hotel with Belgian chef Nic Vanderbeeken. Some ingredients you may not find right away in your local supermarket, but you can get them in any Asian specialty store in (medium) large cities.

1 kg green beans

For the peanut sauce:

6 shallots, shredded
2 garlic cloves, crushed
2 chilli peppers, finely chopped
25 g ginger, finely chopped
1 stick lemongrass, bruised
4 lime leaves
1 teaspoon coriander seeds, cumin, anise seeds finely ground (mixed)
250 g roasted unsalted peanuts, finely ground
1 dl sunflower oil
2 dl mint vinegar (see basic recipe p. 174)
20 ml oyster sauce
1 tablespoon shrimp paste
200 ml sweet soy sauce

To finish:

roasted sesame seeds
pickled shallot rings (see basic recipe p. 174)
a few tufts of fresh mint and coriander

Cook the beans in water with salt and place in ice water to cool.
Lightly fry all the ingredients for the peanut sauce in a pan with oil.
Deglaze with the vinegar and oyster sauce.
Add the shrimp paste and the soy sauce, simmer everything briefly and season to taste.
Leave to cool and mix into the cooked beans.
Finish with sesame seeds, shallot rings and fresh herbs.

Beet puffs, goat cheese, herb salad, nut vinaigrette

Onion compote forms the basis of pissaladière, a well-known savoury pie from the south of France. I use this compote in many dishes. The nut vinaigrette is inspired by a sauce I learned from the famous Roger Souvereyns.

5 red beetroots
5 yellow beetroots

For the compote:

500 g onions, cut into rings
100 g sugar
1 dl sherry vinegar
1 bunch fresh thyme, coarsely chopped
1 garlic clove, crushed
1 dl olive oil
pepper and salt

For the goat cheese:

500 g fresh goat cheese, without crust
100 g candied onion compote
30 g flower honey
20 g fresh chopped thyme leaves, without twigs
fresh-ground pepper

For the nut vinaigrette:

see recipe page 172

To finish:

a herb salad of mint, basil, dill, tarragon and some sourdough croutons
optionally some pickled shallot rings

Lightly cook the ingredients for the compote until they start to colour. Chop finely and season.
Mix the goat cheese with the compote, honey and thyme in a bowl and season with fresh-ground pepper.
Cook the beets for 1½ hours in a preheated oven at 180 °C until al dente. Peel and cut into uneven pieces. Season to taste and finish with some nut vinaigrette (see basic recipe p. 174).
Arrange the cheese on a plate or some bread, distribute the beets on top and finish with some herb salad and possibly croutons and shallot rings.

Roasted aubergine, tomato chutney and Greek yoghurt

For the aubergine:

5 aubergines, cut in half lengthwise and notched
10 sprigs thyme
5 sprigs rosemary
10 garlic cloves
2 dl olive oil
Maldon salt and pepper

For the chutney:

1 kg passata
3 garlic cloves, crushed
2 tablespoons tomato puree
10 shallots, shredded
100 g sugar
1 dl vinegar
1 tablespoon cumin
1 tablespoon coriander powder
2 pieces star anise
1 cinnamon stick
olive oil
pepper and salt

For the Greek yoghurt:

250 g Greek yoghurt
50 g pickled shallot
1 garlic clove, crushed
pepper and salt

To finish:

fresh herb salad
sourdough croutons
basil oil
tapenade of black olives
pickled shallots
za'atar spice mix

Cover the aubergine with the aromatics.
Spice well and bake for 30 minutes at 180 °C in a preheated oven.
Lightly fry the ingredients for the chutney in olive oil. Allow to thicken to sauce consistency and season to taste. Store in the refrigerator.
Mix the yoghurt well with the shallot and the garlic, and season with salt and pepper.
Remove the aromatics from the aubergines.
Add blobs of chutney and yoghurt to the aubergines.
Finish with the fresh herb salad, croutons, basil oil, tapenade, shallots and za'atar.

Baked green asparagus with sourdough, fresh cheese and veal jus vinaigrette

You can eat this dish as a salad, but it also goes well with a little finely sliced raw ham such as coppa.

For the asparagus:

4 green asparagus per person, cleaned (keep the peelings for soup)
25 g butter
25 ml olive oil
4 sprigs thyme
2 garlic cloves, bruised
pepper and salt

For the fresh cheese:

200 g fresh goat curd or yoghurt curd
30 g brunoise of pickled shallot
a dash of sherry vinegar
pepper and salt

For the vinaigrette:

see basic veal jus recipe on p. 177

To finish:

sourdough bread croutons
herb salad (tarragon, chervil, basil, flowers, etc.)

Cook the asparagus al dente and cool in ice water.
Fry the asparagus golden brown in a pan with butter and olive oil. Finish with the thyme and garlic, and season with salt and pepper.
Mix the curd with the shallot and finish with sherry vinegar. Season with pepper and salt.
Serve the asparagus with the cheese. Finish the salad with the vinaigrette, croutons and herb salad.

Fresh goat cheese with a ratatouille chutney

This chutney is also delicious with a terrine of duck liver, or for those who don't eat it for reasons of principle, a nice game pâté.

Ingredients for the ratatouille:

1 kg red bell pepper, cut into small chunks
1 kg yellow bell pepper, cut into small chunks
1 kg courgettes, cut into small chunks
1 kg onion, chopped into small chunks
2 garlic cloves, crushed
1 bunch thyme
1 bunch rosemary
2 kg sugar
grated peel of 1 lemon and 1 orange
32 ml neutral vinegar
150 g pectin
2 pieces star anise
1 g saffron
2 teaspoons anise seed
3 cinnamon sticks
2 dl white wine

Mix all the ingredients together, cover, and put in the refrigerator to marinate overnight.
The next day, boil everything together, skimming regularly.
Leave to cook for another 2 hours on a low heat.
Leave to cool in the refrigerator or divide into preserving jars.
Serve with a slice of fresh goat cheese. Or add a slice of fragrant sourdough bread or French baguette.

White asparagus, mousseline with tarragon and Szechuan pepper, fresh herbs and croutons

Want to turn this asparagus preparation into a complete fish dish? Then serve the asparagus with a piece of steamed salmon.

For the asparagus:

4 asparagus per person, peeled
olive oil
pepper and Maldon salt

For the mousseline reduction (1 litre):

250 ml white wine
250 ml white wine vinegar
5 shallots, cut into small chunks
50 g Szechuan pepper
100 g fresh tarragon
500 ml water
100 g sugar
1 sprig bay and thyme

For the mousseline:

200 ml of the reduction
340 g clarified butter
240 g egg yolk
200 ml cream
salt

To finish:

parsley, finely chopped
chives, finely chopped
fresh croutons

Cook the asparagus al dente in salted water.
Dab well dry and sprinkle with olive oil.
Season with Maldon sea salt and fresh-ground pepper.
Mix the ingredients for the reduction and reduce to half. Sieve and store separately.
Make a mousseline. For this, beat the reduction together with the yolks until nicely bound. Slowly pour in the clarified butter and bind at room temperature.
Finish with the whipped cream and some salt, and store in a warm place.
Serve the asparagus with the mousseline and finish with chopped parsley, finely chopped chives and fresh croutons.

Pissaladière

This is a tasty pie made with candied onions, very popular in the south of France.

For the onions:

500 g shallot, shredded
1 garlic clove, bruised
1 bunch thyme
1 bunch rosemary
1 dl olive oil
1 dl sherry vinegar
50 g sugar
pepper and salt

For the tart:

1 round layer of puff pastry (30 cm in diameter), pricked with a fork
2 baking trays and baking paper

To finish:

olive tapenade
anchovy fillets, in oil
fine Greek basil

Lightly fry the onions with the aromatics under a lid until the onions release their moisture.
Remove the lid and simmer for 1 hour until everything is golden brown.
Leave to cool and chop finely.
Bake the puff pastry between the two baking trays for 20 minutes in a preheated oven at 170 °C until golden brown.
Leave to cool.
Cover the pie with the onions.
Finish with tapenade, anchovy fillet in oil and fine Greek basil.

Quinoa salad and duck confit 'Thai style'

6 duck legs

For the marinade:

3 garlic cloves, crushed
3 lemongrass stalks, finely shredded
2 dl lemongrass and ginger pickling brine (see basic recipe p. 174)
1 dl soy sauce
2 tablespoons ginger powder
1 tablespoon anise seed
1 tablespoon coriander seed
1 dl nam pla fish sauce
2 small chilli peppers
juice of 1 lime
1 shallot, cut into small chunks
1 litre sunflower oil
2 dl apple juice

For the quinoa:

500 g quinoa, pre-cooked
pepper and salt
1 cucumber, de-seeded and cut into small chunks
½ white of leek, in fine chunks
2 shallots, finely shredded
2 carrots, peeled and cut into rounds
100 g roasted cashew nuts, chopped
30 g mint, finely chopped
30 g coriander, chopped

For the vinaigrette:

50 ml mint vinegar
50 ml soy sauce
2 tablespoons fish sauce
juice of 1 lime
300 ml lemongrass oil (see basic recipe p. 172)

To finish:

some mint and coriander leaves
Preparation:
Mix all the marinade ingredients in a blender.

Marinate the duck legs in the marinade overnight in the refrigerator.
The next day place the duck legs with the marinade in a baking pan and cover with a lid. Cook for 4 to 5 hours at 150 °C. Then remove the meat from the legs and chop it finely. Mix with the gravy.
Mix together all the ingredients for the vinaigrette.
Mix the meat with the pre-cooked quinoa, vegetables, nuts and herbs and season with the vinaigrette.
Season with pepper and salt.
Serve lukewarm and finish with mint and coriander leaves.

Burrata with pickled vegetables, tapenade of Kalamata olives, and coppa

Just like you have different types of mozzarella, you also have burrata of good and of lesser quality. Try to avoid the industrially produced type, which is now coming into supermarkets, and opt for a traditional product from a better cheese shop.

50 g Kalamata olive tapenade
2 burrata
fresh-ground pepper
Maldon sea salt
pickled vegetables (red onions, carrots, radishes, see basic recipes p. 174)
10 thin slices of coppa
100 g ciabatta croutons
some young basil leaves
a salad of fresh herbs (tarragon, dill, watercress etc.)
basil oil (see basic recipe p. 175)

For the basil and rocket jus:

100 g basil
100 g rocket
100 g ice cubes
100 ml olive oil
pepper and salt
thyme vinegar (see basic recipe p. 174)

Arrange a spoonful of tapenade in the centre of the plate and place the burrata on top of the tapenade.
Season with fresh-ground pepper and Maldon sea salt.
Place the pickled vegetables around the burrata and distribute the coppa.
Finish with the croutons, basil leaves and herbs.
Mix the ingredients for the jus in a blender and strain through a sieve. Season with pepper and salt.
Drizzle some basil oil and jus around the preparation.

Fish
-
Poultry
-
Meat

Southern meat balls with fresh thyme, tomato and basil

- INGREDIENTS FOR 10 PEOPLE -

For the meat balls:

1 kg minced veal
40 g thyme, freshly chopped
2 garlic cloves, crushed
150 g parmesan, grated
fresh-ground pepper
salt
3 eggs
150 g breadcrumbs

For the oriental vinegar:

2 litres of pickling brine (basic recipe: 3 litres water, 3 litres vinegar, 2 kg sugar)
50 g fresh ginger, peeled and cut into blocks
50 g lemongrass, cut into pieces
20 g allspice
2 garlic cloves, crushed
25 g fresh coriander
25 g fresh mint

For the basil oil:

1 bunch basil (leaves only)
1 litre sunflower oil
2 garlic cloves, crushed

For the basil sauce:

200 g egg white
150 g basil leaves
1 teaspoon green food dye (optional)
pepper, salt and a little sugar
75 g sharp mustard (e.g. Tierenteyn)
2 garlic cloves, crushed
70 ml sherry vinegar
1 litre sunflower oil
1 dl water

For the tomato chutney:

1 kg tomato passata
3 garlic cloves, crushed
10 shallots, finely shredded
100 g sugar
1 dl oriental vinegar (e.g. mirin)
1 tablespoon cumin
1 tablespoon coriander powder
2 pieces star anise
1 cinnamon stick
pepper and salt
olive oil

To finish:

fresh herbs (mint, basil, coriander, etc.)
grated parmesan

Mix together all the ingredients for the meat balls. Roll out the mixture into 25-gram balls and bake for 8 minutes in a preheated oven at 180 °C.
Bring the oriental pickling brine to the boil, pour in the herbs and spices, leave to cool and strain before use.
Lightly fry all the ingredients for the chutney in some olive oil. Cook on a low heat for 3 hours and season with salt and pepper to taste.
Blend the ingredients for the oil very finely and leave to cool.
Then make the sauce: briefly mix the egg whites with the herbs, mustard, garlic and vinegar in a blender to avoid discolouring the basil.
Work up with some oil and add a little water if the sauce is too firm.
Prepare a salad of fresh herbs with basil oil and oriental vinegar.
Serve the meat balls with the salad, sauce and chutney and finish with some grated parmesan.

Lamb meatballs with celeriac, sesame and cauliflower

For the lamb meatballs:

500 g minced veal
500 g minced lamb
100 g fresh coriander
2 tablespoons cumin powder
2 garlic cloves, crushed
150 g parmesan, grated
ground pepper
3 eggs
150 g breadcrumbs

For the celeriac:

1 kg celeriac, peeled and chopped into little cubes
200 g shallot, shredded
2 garlic cloves, crushed
½ lemon on salt, cut into small pieces
50 g fresh ginger, peeled
1 lemongrass stalk
2 tablespoons cumin powder
1 dl olive oil
40 g honey
1 dl white wine
4 dl chicken bouillon
200 g sesame paste
juice of 2 limes
pepper and salt

For the cauliflower:

1 cauliflower, cut into pieces
pepper and salt
1 dl olive oil
grated peel of 1 lemon
50 g pickled shallot

For the candied shallot:

500 g shallot, finely shredded
olive oil

To finish:

fresh yoghurt with pickled onions and garlic (see p. 174)
a few sprigs of leaf parsley
pickled raisins (see p. 174)
basil oil (see basic recipe p. 175)

Mix the minced meat with the other meatball ingredients. Roll into balls of around 30 grams each. Bake the meatballs until golden brown in a preheated oven at 180 °C.
Lightly fry the celeriac with the other ingredients in olive oil.
Add the honey and deglaze with the wine and bouillon.
Cook the celeriac and then leave to boil to reduce the liquid by half. Mix everything finely in a blender with the sesame paste and lime juice. Season with pepper and salt.
Store in the refrigerator until ready to use.
Mix the cauliflower finely in a blender and season with pepper, salt, olive oil and grated lemon peel. Mix with the shallot.
Lightly fry the shallots with the olive oil until they caramelize.
Finish the celeriac and cauliflower with them.Serve with the meatballs.
Finish with the suggestions from the list of ingredients, to taste.

STAUB

Oriental meatballs, beans with sesame and miso

For the beans:

1 kg fine beans, cleaned
1 tablespoon sesame seeds, roasted
2 tablespoons nam pla fish sauce
2 tablespoons mint vinegar (see basic recipe p. 174)
2 tablespoons oriental oil (see basic recipe p. 174)
½ small chilli pepper, finely chopped
grated peel of 1 lime
a few pickled shallot rings
5 sprigs fresh coriander and mint

For the miso sauce:

1 dl water
2 garlic cloves, crushed
75 g blond miso
2 tablespoons soy sauce
2 tablespoons roasted sesame oil
200 g egg white
80 ml sushi vinegar
pepper and salt
1 litre sunflower oil

For the meatballs:

1 kg minced veal
50 g coriander, finely chopped
50 g spring onion, finely chopped
100 g cashew nuts, roasted and chopped
grated peel of 2 limes
2 tablespoons fish sauce
1 tablespoon ginger powder
2 garlic cloves, crushed
pinch of chilli pepper
3 eggs
150 g breadcrumbs

First make the miso sauce. Mix all the ingredients except the sunflower oil in a blender until smooth, then pour in the oil slowly and bind.
Blanch the beans in salted water, cool them in ice water and cook them with the remaining ingredients. Finish with the grated lime peel, shallot rings and coriander.
Mix the minced meat with the other meatball ingredients and roll the mixture into balls. Bake until done in a preheated oven at 180 °C.
Pour some miso dressing on a plate and arrange a few balls on it. Serve with the bean salad.

Spring roll with smoked eel, miso and soy

For the vegetables, follow your imagination. Stay with the season and only use vegetables that you can easily cut into a julienne. This doesn't work with tomatoes or avocados, for example.

For the spring rolls:

5 sheets rice paper
10 fresh coriander and mint leaves
60 g julienne of carrot, cucumber, leek, Chinese cabbage, pumpkin or other seasonal vegetables per spring roll
salt and pepper
90 g smoked eel fillet per spring roll
brine (see basic recipe p. 174)

For the miso sauce:

1 dl water
2 garlic cloves, crushed
75 g blond miso
2 tablespoons soy sauce
2 tablespoons roasted oil
200 g egg white
80 ml sushi vinegar
pepper and salt
1 litre sunflower oil

To finish:

roasted sesame seeds

Soak the rice paper in cold water until nice and flexible.
Marinate the vegetables and fresh herbs for 20 minutes in the brine and season with salt and pepper.
Place all the ingredients on the rice sheet and roll tightly.
Cover the rolled rice sheets and leave for 1 hour in the refrigerator. That way you can cut the spring rolls more easily.
Now prepare the miso sauce: mix all the ingredients except the sunflower oil in a blender. Pour in the sunflower oil slowly and bind like you would a runny mayonnaise.
Finish with a few roasted sesame seeds.

Chicken curry

This recipe is based on Sri Lankan cuisine. Coconut milk is often used here, as in the southern states of India, along with other spices from the rest of India: curry, cumin, cardamom etc. In place of chicken you can also make this dish with prawns.

6 onions, diced
3 tablespoons garlic, chopped
1 small fresh chilli pepper, finely chopped
3 tablespoons ginger, chopped
1 tablespoon coriander powder
1 tablespoon turmeric powder
1 tablespoon curry
1 tablespoon cumin powder
a neutral oil like sunflower oil
2 cinnamon sticks
4 cardamom pods
4 cloves
3 tomatoes, de-seeded and cut into small pieces
2 tablespoons tomato concentrate
1 litre coconut milk
1 kg farm chicken fillet, cut into little pieces
lemongrass oil (see basic recipe p. 172)
6 tablespoons coriander, finely chopped
juice and grated peel of 2 limes

To finish:

steamed rice
snow peas

Lightly fry the onion, garlic, chilli pepper and ginger in the oil.
Add the spices and simmer for a while.
Add the tomato pieces and tomato concentrate and leave to simmer slowly for 10 minutes.
Moisten with the coconut milk and only now add the chicken chunks.
Leave to simmer for 20 minutes until the chicken is done. Finish with the lime juice.
Finish with fresh coriander, lemongrass oil and grated lime peel.
Serve with steamed rice and boiled snow peas with coriander.

Candied duck leg, green olive and date chutney, herb salad and fresh yoghurt, and couscous with herbs

For the duck legs:

4 duck legs
2 dl meat marinade (see ribeye recipe p. XX)
2 dl apple juice

For the chutney:

500 g onion, shredded
2 garlic cloves, crushed
one sprig each of thyme, sage and rosemary
2 dl olive oil
250 g green olive tapenade
250 g Medjool dates, stoned and chopped
200 g honey
2 dl sherry vinegar
2 dl white wine
20 ml orange blossom water
juice of 1 lime
pepper and salt

For the couscous:

150 g fine couscous
500 ml vegetable bouillon
1 piece star anise
1 garlic clove, crushed
a few saffron threads
1 cinnamon stick
1 tablespoon cumin
1 tablespoon chicken bouillon powder
1 dl olive oil
grated peel and juice of 1 lime
pepper and salt

For the yoghurt with pickled shallot:

250 g Greek yoghurt
50 g pickled shallot
pepper and salt

For the herb salad:

mixture of fresh rocket, mint, coriander, chervil and tarragon

Place the duck legs in a roasting pan and marinate them in the marinade. Sprinkle with the apple juice and cover with aluminium foil.
Cook the legs in the oven at 140 °C for 3 hours until nicely candied and tender.
Now prepare the chutney. Lightly fry the onion and garlic with herbs in the olive oil. Add the tapenade and Medjool dates and leave to simmer together for 10 minutes. Add the honey. Deglaze with the vinegar and white wine and simmer for another 10 minutes until all the moisture has evaporated. Finish with the orange blossom water and lime juice and season with salt and pepper.
For the couscous, bring the bouillon with all the aromatics to the boil and boil gently for 10 minutes. Spread the couscous on a flat plate with a raised edge and pour the bouillon over it. Cover and leave the couscous to absorb all the moisture. Finish with the olive oil, grated lime peel and lime juice, and season with salt and pepper. Finely chop the salad herbs and sprinkle over the couscous.
Serve the duck leg in a dish and finish with a few blobs of chutney.
Serve the couscous and yoghurt separately.

Candied pork cheek with tarragon, wild garlic, candied potato and beans

For the pork cheeks:

1 pork cheek per person
1 knob butter
1 bundle fresh thyme
2 onions and 2 carrots, in mirepoix
1 bundle fresh tarragon
2 garlic cloves, crushed
pepper and salt
5 dl red wine
1 tablespoon brown sugar
1 tablespoon mustard
veal stock to moisten

For the tarragon emulsion:

200 g gastrique with tarragon
240 g egg yolks
340 g clarified butter
200 ml cream
salt to taste

For the beans:

40 g beans per person
wild garlic oil (see basic recipe p. 175)
1 onion, brunoised
1 sprig thyme
pepper and salt
pinch of sugar
knob of butter
olive oil

For the potatoes:

1 potato per person
goose fat
2 garlic cloves
a few sprigs of thyme
knob of butter

To finish:

a herb salad
thyme vinegar
basil oil (see basic recipe p. 175)

Lightly fry the cheeks in the butter. Add the vegetables and herbs, and season with salt and pepper. Deglaze with the red wine. Add the sugar and mustard and then pour in the veal stock until the cheeks are covered.

Leave to cook until nice and soft.

Pour off the gravy and reduce by half in a separate pan.

Mix the ingredients for the tarragon emulsion for 10 minutes at 80 °C in a Thermomix. Pour the mixture into an espuma bottle with two gas cartridges.

Prick out round shapes from the potatoes and vacuum cook for 20 minutes at 90 °C in goose fat with garlic and thyme. Leave to cool and fry lightly in a knob of butter before serving.

Blanch the beans briefly in boiling salted water and cool in ice water. Season with wild garlic oil.

Stew the brunoise of onions in the butter and mix with the beans. Add the sprig of thyme, pepper and salt, and a pinch of sugar.

Serve the cheeks with the sauce, potatoes, beans and tarragon emulsion. Serve with a fresh herb salad, seasoned with basil oil and thyme vinegar.

Sea bass baked in its skin with mango, tomato, chilli and ginger

4 sea bass fillets of 100 g per person, filleted, with skin
Maldon sea salt
1 mango, peeled and cut into chunks
10 cherry tomatoes, halved
20 g ginger, cut into small pieces
pinch fresh chilli

1 dl lemongrass oil (see basic recipe p. 172)
pinch of sugar
grated peel and juice of 2 limes
salt
3 sprigs fresh coriander, finely chopped
oriental vinegar (of chilli and lemongrass, see basic recipe p. 174)

To finish:

basil sauce (see basic recipe p. 175)
some basil leaves

Bake the sea bass on the skin side in a non-stick pan or on a griddle.
Season right before serving with Maldon sea salt and the grated peel of one lime.
Mix the mango with the cherry tomatoes, ginger and chilli, and add a dash of lemongrass oil.
Season with the sugar, lime juice, salt, fresh coriander and a dash of oriental vinegar.
Place the garnish on the plate and place the fish on the garnish.
Serve with some basil sauce and finish with some basil leaves.

Tagliata of Black Angus ribeye, roast potatoes, rosemary, rocket, balsamic vinegar

For the marinade:

3 garlic cloves, crushed
6 sprigs fresh thyme, finely chopped
2 dl thyme pickling brine (see basic recipe p. 174)
1 dl soy sauce
2 tablespoons cumin powder, anise seed, coriander seed (mixed)
1 shallot, shredded
juice of 1 lime
1 litre sunflower oil

For the tagliata:

1 x 250 g ribeye (for 2 people)
1 bunch fine rocket
50 g parmesan
balsamic vinegar
olive oil
truffle mayonnaise (see toast with beef carpaccio p. 50)

For the potatoes:

60 g Belle de Fontenay potatoes per person, unpeeled and cut into pieces
olive oil
2 garlic cloves, bruised
2 sprigs rosemary
freshly ground pepper
Maldon sea salt

First mix the ingredients for the marinade in a blender and keep in a cool place.
Heat the meat in the oven at 55 °C. Then bake on both sides on the grill. Cook to taste (raw to well-done) or leave in the still warm oven.
Place the meat back on the grill just before serving and coat with the marinade.
Roll the potato chunks through the olive oil, garlic and rosemary, and season with salt and pepper, then bake golden brown and keep warm in the oven.
Cut the meat into thin slices and place on a large plate for 2 people.
Season with Maldon sea salt and coarse pepper.
Arrange the rocket on the meat. Finish with balsamic vinegar, olive oil and grated parmesan.
Serve the potatoes and the mayonnaise separately.

Jumbo mussels with dill juice and smoked haddock

For the mussels:

1 kg jumbo mussels
1 onion, in chunks
1 celery stalk, cut into chunks
2 garlic cloves, crushed
1 dl white wine
4 sprigs dill

For the jus:

2 onions, in mirepoix
1 stalk white celery
1 garlic clove, crushed
200 g smoked haddock
1 dl white wine
3 dl mussel fluid
1 litre fish fumet
6 sprigs dill
dill vinegar (see basic recipe p. 174)
200 g butter

To finish:

a few tufts of dill, sourdough croutons and leek oil (see basic recipe p. 174)

Briefly fry the mussels in a wide pan with the vegetables and aromatics, and reserve the juice.
Now prepare the jus. Lightly fry the onion, celery and garlic in a pot.
Add the haddock and simmer together for a while.
Deglaze with white wine and leave to reduce.
Add the fish fumet and the mussel juice and leave to reduce by half.
Pour the mixture through a sieve onto the dill sprigs and leave briefly to infuse.
Finish with the dill vinegar and fresh cold butter.
Before serving, mix with a hand blender into a frothy sauce.
Distribute the sauce over the mussels.
Finish with small pieces of dill, sourdough croutons and leek oil.

Chicken drumsticks, hoisin sauce, coleslaw, cashew nuts

For the brine: 80 g salt per 1 litre water
4 chicken legs, boned, with skin
peanut oil

For the hoisin sauce:

ketchup
soy sauce
oyster sauce
fresh ginger, finely chopped
sriracha
lemongrass oil (see basic recipe p. 172)

And also:

200 g coleslaw (a mixture of red and white cabbage), shredded using a mandolin slicer
20 g white sesame seeds, roasted
20 g unsalted cashew nuts, roasted
50 g spring onion, finely chopped
chilli and lemongrass vinegar (see basic recipe p. 174)
lemongrass oil
grated peel of 1 lime
8 fresh mint leaves

First make a brine. Take 80 grams of salt per litre of water.
Marinate the chicken legs for 20 minutes in the brine.
Rinse well and vacuum cook for 30 minutes at 62 °C.
Leave the legs to cool and then bake in the pan with the peanut oil until crispy.
Make a mixture of the ingredients for the hoisin sauce, to taste and to the desired spiciness.
Brush the baked legs with the hoisin sauce.
Mix the coleslaw with the other ingredients and arrange some coleslaw on each chicken leg.

Neck of lamb with carrots, ginger chutney, pink pepper and pine nuts

For the neck of lamb:

3 kg neck of lamb
olive oil
pepper and salt
1 carrot, peeled and cut into rounds
1 onion, peeled and cut into small pieces
3 pieces star anise
1 teaspoon cardamom
1 tablespoon cumin
1 tablespoon curry
1 small chilli pepper, diced
1 tablespoon cumin powder
1 candied lemon, cut into pieces
2 garlic cloves, crushed
juice of 1 lime
2 litres chicken bouillon
butter
1 bunch of thyme
1 bunch of sage

For the chutney:

250 g shallot, finely shredded
50 g pink pepper
2 garlic cloves, crushed
100 g pine seeds, roasted
50 g ginger, finely chopped
3 lime leaves
juice of 2 limes
1 tablespoon chicken bouillon powder
2 tablespoons curry
2 dl oriental vinegar (see basic recipe p. 174)
2 dl lemongrass oil (see basic recipe p. 172)

For the carrot puree:

1 kg carrots, peeled and cut into rounds
butter
1 garlic clove, crushed
2 onions, cut into small pieces
2 tablespoons curry
2 lime leaves
2 sprigs bay leaves
2 dl chicken bouillon
pepper and salt

To finish:

orange oil (see basic recipe p. 174)
fresh coriander tufts
a few sprigs of leaf parsley

Lightly fry the neck of lamb in olive oil and season with salt and pepper.
Fry the garnish lightly in a stewing pot and add the necks.
Deglaze with the lime juice and moisten with the bouillon.
Leave the meat to stew slowly until you can prick it through with a fork.
Drain the gravy and reduce to half.
Leave the meat to cool and roll in plastic wrap. Store in the refrigerator.
Cut thick slices from the meat and fry in butter with some thyme and sage.
Finish with the gravy.
Lightly fry all the ingredients for the chutney in the lemongrass oil. Leave to candy lightly and reduce to marmalade consistency. Leave to cool.
Lightly fry the carrots in the butter with the aromatics.
Deglaze with bouillon and leave to simmer. Continue cooking and remove the bay leaves and lime leaves. Mix in a blender and season with salt and pepper.
Finish the preparation with a dash of orange oil and a few tufts of coriander and leaf parsley.

Cod, mashed potato and bouillabaisse jus

4 x 120 g pieces of cod
sunflower oil
2 piquillo peppers
basil vinegar
basil oil (see basic recipe p. 175)
pepper and salt
a dash of pastis

For the mashed potato:

4 large Bintje-type potatoes
200 ml olive oil
ground pepper
1 teaspoon anise seed
1 shallot, finely shredded

For the bouillabaisse jus:

1/2 fennel, cut into pieces
2 onions, cut into pieces
2 carrots, peeled and cut into rounds
3 garlic cloves, crushed
1 small bunch of thyme and bay leaves
pinch of saffron
1 dl white wine
1 kg of fish for the fish soup (ask your fishmonger what is in stock)
2 tablespoons tomato concentrate
1 bouillon cube
olive oil
butter

To finish:

fennel leaves
basil sprouts

Fry the cod pieces golden brown on both sides in a hot pan.
Marinate the peppers with some balsamic vinegar and basil oil.
Peel the potatoes and cut into large chunks, then boil them in salted water, drain and dry in the same pan.
Mash the potatoes and add the oil, season with pepper and anise seed, and finish with the shallot.
Now prepare the jus. Lightly fry the vegetables with the aromatics and deglaze with the white wine.
Fry the fish in a pan and deglaze with the pastis.
Put everything together in a cooking pot with the fish fumet and bring to the boil.
Add the bouillon cube and tomato concentrate.
Leave to simmer gently for 2 hours. Then mix with a hand blender and pour through a sieve.
Work up with olive oil and some butter.
Place the mashed potato in the middle of a plate. Place the fish on the potato and finish with fennel leaves, a few basil shoots and the piquillo pepper.

Vitello tonnato

- INGREDIENTS, TO SERVE 4 -

For the veal:

500 g roasted veal
1 garlic clove
2 sprigs fresh thyme, rosemary and sage
2 dl olive oil
1 dl balsamic vinegar
pepper and salt

For the sauce:

200 g egg white
2 garlic cloves
1 dl olive oil
50 g green olive tapenade
50 g capers in their juice
100 g canned tuna
2 tablespoons mustard
pepper and salt
a pinch of sugar
sherry vinegar
1 litre salad oil

To finish:

fried capers, fine bread croutons, grated parmesan, rocket

Place the veal with the aromatics in a vacuum bag. Leave to marinate overnight.
Cook the next day for 1 hour at 59°C.
Cool in ice water.
Cut into paper-thin slices and arrange on a plate.
Mix the egg whites finely with the garlic and the other aromatics.
Pour slowly into the oil and bind into a rich, runny sauce.
Pour the sauce generously over the meat.
Finish with fried capers, fine bread croutons, grated parmesan and rocket.

Poussin chickens with tarragon, candied shallot and carrot, and radicchio (Italian chicory)

4 poussin (baby) chickens
1 bunch tarragon
4 garlic cloves, bruised
pepper and salt
1 dl olive oil
200 g fresh butter

For the jus:

4 shallots, finely diced
2 garlic cloves, crushed
olive oil
1 dl cognac
2 dl white wine
5 dl chicken bouillon
2 dl cream
ground pepper
salt
tarragon oil (see basic recipe p. 174)
cornflour
tarragon, finely chopped

For the shallots:

1 garlic clove, crushed
100 g butter
olive oil
sugar
pepper and salt
8 thick shallots, cut in half lengthwise
2 sprigs of thyme

For the carrots:

4 thick carrots in different colours, peeled and cleaned
1 shallot, cut into small chunks
2 garlic cloves, crushed
100 g butter
olive oil
1 star anise
2 sprigs of bay and thyme
pepper and salt
sugar
2 cloves
1 litre chicken bouillon
50 g parsley, finely chopped

Stuff the poussin chickens with tarragon and a clove of garlic. Season with pepper and salt.
Pour oil over the chickens and place a knob of butter on each.
Cook in a preheated oven at 180°C for 45 minutes.
For the jus, lightly fry the shallots in a pan, add the garlic and deglaze with the cognac and the white wine.
Reduce and then add the bouillon and the cream.
Reduce by half and season with pepper, salt and tarragon oil.
Thicken the sauce with cornflour. Add some freshly chopped tarragon before serving.
Then prepare the shallots. Melt the butter and the olive oil in a pan with the garlic. Add sugar, pepper and salt and place the shallots flat-side down in the butter. Add the sprigs of thyme and place a sheet of baking paper on the shallots. Cover with a lid and leave the shallots to cook nicely in the same way as endives.
Cut the carrots into thick pieces.
Cook them with the shallot, garlic and aromatics in a shallow pot and moisten with the bouillon.
Cover with a lid and leave to cook until the carrots are nice and soft.
Remove the carrots from the pot and leave the liquid to reduce.
Glaze the carrots in the pan with butter. Finish with chopped parsley.
Serve this dish with potato mousseline or pasta and a salad of radicchio enriched with thyme vinegar and basil oil (see basic recipes p. 175).

Sweets

Vanilla ice cream, chocolate emulsion, cookie crunch

For the ice cream:

12 egg yolks
140 g sugar
1 litre milk
2 vanilla pods
50 ml cream
pinch of salt

For the chocolate emulsion:

500 ml cream
25 g sugar
225 g pure chocolate
50 g milk chocolate
250 g egg white
pinch of salt

For the crunch:

450 g soft butter
200 g icing sugar
500 g flour
150 g dark chocolate in small pieces
3 egg yolks
pinch of salt

To finish:

olive oil
Maldon sea salt

For the ice cream, beat the egg yolks with the sugar. Heat the milk with the vanilla pods. Combine everything, mix and heat to 83 °C. Sieve, add the cream and finish with a pinch of salt. Churn into ice cream in the ice turbine.

For the emulsion, bring the cream with the sugar to the boil and pour onto the milk and pure chocolate. Beat and add the egg white. Season with a pinch of salt and mix well. Pour the chocolate mixture into an espuma bottle with two gas cartridges. Keep warm in a bain-marie at 60 °C.

Then bake the cookies. Mix all the ingredients. Form a thick roll of the mixture and wrap in plastic wrap. Leave to stiffen and then cut into 1 cm thick pieces. Bake the cookies for 20 minutes at 165 °C in a preheated oven.

Finish with a splash of olive oil and a few flakes of Maldon sea salt.

Coconut panna cotta with pineapple

For the panna cotta (80 g per person):

600 g coconut milk
100 g white chocolate
2 gelatine leaves

For the pineapple:

½ pineapple, cut into pieces
2 tablespoons sugar syrup
leaves of 3 sprigs of fresh mint, finely chopped
80 ml brown rum
juice and grated peel of 1 lime

For the coconut espuma:

400 ml coconut milk
30 g glucose
120 g sugar
400 ml milk
120 ml cream
9 ml brown rum
3 gelatine leaves

For the coconut crumble:

500 g soft butter
500 g grated coconut
500 g sugar
500 g flour

To finish:

grated peel of 1 lime

For the panna cotta, heat up the coconut milk and pour it over the chocolate. Soak the gelatine leaves in cold water, squeeze them out and add them to the coconut milk with the chocolate. Divide the mixture into little glasses and leave to cool.
Mix the pineapple with the syrup, mint, rum and lime and divide the mixture between the panna cotta glasses.
Heat the ingredients for the espuma. Soak the gelatine leaves in cold water, squeeze them out and add to the mixture. Stir and pour everything into an espuma bottle with two gas cartridges.
For the coconut crumble, bake the grated coconut with the butter, sugar and flour in a preheated oven at 170 °C until golden brown. Mix the crumble every 5 minutes.
Serve the panna cotta with the pineapple, espuma, some grated lime peel and the crumble.

Lemon tart with white chocolate and raspberries

Precision is essential in patisserie. Resist the temptation to round up or down the amounts in this recipe, as this may give a less successful end result.

For 1 tart:

8 cm tart base
cocoa butter
250 g raspberries
icing sugar

For the crémeux of white chocolate with lemon:

74 g glucose
66 g egg yolks
162 ml milk
570 ml cream
288 g white chocolate
juice of 3 lemons
grated peel of 1 lime, 1 lemon, 1 orange
pinch of saffron
2 cinnamon sticks
2 gelatine leaves

Coat a tart base with cocoa butter and leave to stiffen.
Heat the glucose and add to the yolks. Mix well.
Bring the milk to the boil with the cream, the chocolate, aromatics and spices. Add the egg yolk mixture and bring to a temperature of 82 °C. Remove the cinnamon sticks from the mixture.
Pour through a fine sieve and add the soaked and squeezed gelatine. Stir and pour the filling into the tart base. Leave to stiffen in the refrigerator.
Arrange the raspberries nicely on the cake and finish with icing sugar.

Carrot cake

115 g soft butter
120 g brown sugar
100 g white sugar
2 eggs
40 ml sunflower oil
200 g flour
4 g baking powder
1.5 g bicarbonate of soda
1.5 g cinnamon powder
5 g salt
225 g carrot, grated

Preheat the oven to 170 °C.
Beat the butter and sugar together into a homogeneous, blond-coloured mass.
Then fold in the other ingredients.
Fill a greased cake tin with the batter and bake in the preheated oven for 45 minutes.

Heart waffles with whipped cream

1 vanilla pod
750 ml milk, lukewarm
40 g yeast
120 ml water, lukewarm
300 g butter, melted
900 g flour
4 eggs
pinch of salt

To finish:

icing sugar
freshly whipped cream

Leave the vanilla pod to infuse in the milk.
Add the yeast to the water and milk and stir well.
Sift the flour and fold well into the liquid.
Now add the eggs and the melted butter, and mix with a hand blender.
Add the salt.
Leave the batter to cool for 3 hours in the refrigerator.
Bake heart-shaped waffles and finish with icing sugar.
Serve with freshly whipped cream.

Chocolate tart with sea salt, hazelnut praliné and coffee

- INGREDIENTS FOR ONE TART FOR 6 TO 8 PEOPLE-

8 cm tart base
cocoa butter

For the salted caramel:

480 g sugar
50 ml water
400 ml cream
80 g cold fresh butter
28 g Maldon sea salt

For the ganache:

180 g hazelnut praliné
180 g pure chocolate
70 g salted caramel
220 ml cream

To finish:

100 g hazelnuts, broken and roasted
freshly whipped cream
icing sugar

Caramelize the sugar and deglaze with water.
Heat the cream and pour onto the sugar water.Add butter and salt.
Mix, sieve and leave to cool.
Soften the praliné to prevent lumping.Stir in the chocolate and salted caramel.
Heat the cream and pour over the mixture. Mix well.
Coat the tart base with cocoa butter and leave to stiffen.
Add the ganache up to the edge.
Sprinkle some hazelnuts over the tart.
Serve with whipped cream and icing sugar.

Basic Recipes

Mustard vinaigrette

Ingredients:
150 g soft mustard
1 garlic clove, crushed
3 tablespoons sherry vinegar
pepper and salt
a pinch of sugar
100 ml water
1 litre sunflower oil

Preparation:
Mix all ingredients except the oil in a blender, and then pour in the sunflower oil and blend together.

Lemongrass oil

Ingredients:
1 litre sunflower oil
2 garlic cloves, crushed
1 small chilli pepper
50 g fresh ginger, peeled and cut into pieces
100 g lemongrass stalks, finely chopped

Preparation:
Heat the oil to 80 °C and then mix all the ingredients together in a blender. Then pour everything through a fine sieve and leave to cool.

Oriental vinegar

Ingredients:
1 litre pickling brine
50 g ginger, cut into pieces
50 g lemongrass, cut into pieces
50 g fresh coriander, minced
3 cloves of garlic, crushed
2 chilli peppers
3 lime leaves

Preparation:
Bring the pickling brine to the boil and pour it onto the herbs. Cover and leave to cool.

Pickling brine from fresh herbs

In this book, we often work with pickled vegetables or herbs. You need a basic brine for that. You can make it easily this way:

Ingredients:
1 litre water
1 litre vinegar
500 g sugar
500 g of fresh herbs such as mint, thyme or sage

Preparation:
Mix the water with the vinegar and the sugar and bring to the boil. Then pour onto the fresh herbs, leave to cool and pour through a sieve before use.
You can use both the brine and the vegetables or herbs that you use in the brine. In the book we do this for example with shallot.

Basil oil

Nota bene: This is the pure basic recipe. For emulsions, other ingredients are needed.

Ingredients:
1 bunch basil (only the leaves)
1 litre sunflower oil
2 garlic cloves, crushed

Preparation:
Mix everything very finely in a blender and store in a cool place.

We also use leek oil in this book. You make this in a different way: heat the sunflower oil to 80 °C and only then mix in 400 grams of green leek (cut into pieces). Strain through a fine sieve and store in a cool place.

Meat marinade

Ingredients:
3 garlic cloves
6 sprigs fresh thyme, minced
2 dl thyme pickling brine
1 dl soy sauce
4 tablespoons smoked paprika powder
1 tablespoon cumin and aniseed
1 shallot, diced
1 litre sunflower oil

Preparation:
Mix everything very finely in a blender.

Pasta dough

Ingredients:
1 kg fine-ground pasta flour
20 ml neutral vinegar
pinch of salt
960 g egg yolks

Preparation:
Mix all ingredients with a dough hook and leave for 2 hours. Then work the dough to the desired pasta shape.

Veal jus

This jus or stock forms the basis of many sauces that we use in this book.

Ingredients:
5 kg veal bones
1 kg onion, in mirepoix
500 g carrots, in mirepoix
300 g flour
1 bunch thyme
4 garlic cloves, bruised
1 litre red port

Preparation:
Roast the bones in the oven at 210 °C until golden brown. Add the vegetables and sauté them. Add the flour and cook for 10 minutes.
Skim off the fat and place everything in a cooking pot. Add the thyme, garlic and port, and then water until everything is covered. Bring to the boil and leave to cook gently for 12 hours. Pour through a sieve and reduce to a jus.

Organic sourdough bread with spelt and seeds

Many salads and other preparations are served with sourdough croutons. Other dishes are meant to be served on a slice of sourdough bread.
This is a recipe for 6 small sourdough loaves.

Ingredients:
1420 g organic white flour, 65%
365 g organic spelt flour, 65%
365 g mixed sunflower and pumpkin seeds
350 g sourdough
1.5 litres water
40 g salt

Preparation:
Put all the ingredients in the food processor bowl. Insert a kneading hook in the machine and let it run for 5 minutes at position 1, and then 7 minutes at maximum speed.
Do you knead the bread by hand? Then fold it in half every half hour. Take the side of the bread and fold it to the centre. Repeat four times. Make sure the ambient temperature does not exceed 23 to 24 °C.
Dust the work surface with flour. Remove the dough from the bowl with wet hands and place it on the work surface. Cover with a damp tea towel. Leave to rest for 30 minutes.
Divide the dough into six and shape loaves. Place in the refrigerator overnight.
Preheat the oven to 250 °C.
Score the bread with a sharp knife. Bake the bread for 10 minutes at 250 °C and 25 minutes at 200 °C. The core must be at 90 °C.
Leave the bread to cool.

Index

P

Q

R

S

T

V

W

Y

Z

Welkin & Meraki Brussels

Colophon

welkinandmeraki.com

Benoit and Bernard Dewitte
Beertegemstraat 52
9750 Zingem
09/384.56.52.
benoitdewitte.be

wwww.lannoo.com

Register on our web site and we will regularly send you a newsletter with information about new books and interesting, exclusive offers.

Text: Benoit Dewitte and Toni De Coninck
Photography: Heikki Verdurme, Thomas De Bruyne (p. 8,10,11,14,28,29)
Graphic design: Jessy Van Durme
Translation: Michael Lomax

If you have observations or questions, please contact our editorial office:
redactielifestyle@lannoo.com

D/2019/45/564 – NUR 440
ISBN 978 94 014 6502 1

Thanks to:

Indu+ - Olivier Taillieu
www.induplus.eu

Objet Trouvé
www.objet-trouve.be

Benoit Viaene
www.benoitviaene.be

WEIGHTS FOR DRY INGREDIENTS

20g	¾ oz
25g	1 oz
40g	1½oz
50g	2oz
60g	2½oz
75g	3oz
100g	3½oz
125g	4oz
150g	5oz
175g	6oz
200g	7oz
225g	8oz
250g	9oz
300g	11oz
350g	12oz
400g	14oz
450g	1lb
500g	1lb 2oz
550g	1¼lb
600g	1lb 5oz
650g	1lb 7oz
700g	1lb 9oz
750g	1lb 11oz
800g	1¾lb
900g	2lb
1kg	2¼lb

LIQUID MEASURES

METRIC	IMPERIAL	US
25ml	1fl oz	
50ml	2fl oz	¼ cup
75ml	3fl oz	
100ml	3½fl oz	
120ml	4fl oz	½ cup
150ml	5fl oz	
175ml	6fl oz	¾ cup
200ml	7fl oz	
250ml	8fl oz	1 cup
300ml	10fl oz/½ pint	1¼ cups
400ml	14fl oz	
450ml	15fl oz	2 cups/1 pint
600ml	1 pint	2½ cups
750ml	1¼ pints	
900ml	1½ pints	
1 litre	1¾ pints	1 quart

OVEN TEMPERATURES

°C	°F
110	225
120	250
140	275
150	300
160	325
180	350
190	375
200	400
220	425
230	450
240	475